KINGDOM LIFE THAT Lasts

AN OVERVIEW OF 1 AND 2 SAMUEL

JACK HAYFORD
SCOTT BAUER • JACK HAMILTON

KINGDOM LIFE THAT LASTS
A Practical, Introductory Guidebook for a
Comprehensive Overview in the Bible Books
of First and Second Samuel

Published by Living Way Ministries
14800 Sherman Way
Van Nuys, CA (USA) 91405-2499
(818) 779-8400 • (800) 776-8180

ISBN 0-916847-27-6
Printed in the United States of America.

TABLE OF CONTENTS

If this is your first use of the Bible Book-a-Month study guide, read pages 67-68.

	FIRST SAMUEL	SECOND SAMUEL
KEY WORD	TRANSITION	DAVID
KEY CHAPTERS	FIRST SAMUEL 15	SECOND SAMUEL 11
KEY VERSES	FIRST SAMUEL 15:22 *"So Samuel said:* *'Has the Lord as great delight in burnt offerings and sacrifices, as in obeying the voice of the Lord? Behold, to obey is better than sacrifice, and to heed than the fat of rams.'"*	SECOND SAMUEL 7:12–13 *"When your days are fulfilled and you rest with your fathers, I will set up your seed after you, who will come from your body, and I will establish his kingdom.* *"He shall build a house for My name, and I will establish the throne of his kingdom forever."*

INTRODUCING THE BIBLE BOOK OF
1 SAMUEL

Author:	Uncertain
Date:	Between 931 and 722 B.C.
Theme:	God Is Working In History
Key Persons:	Samuel, Saul, David

AUTHOR

The author of 1 Samuel is not named in this book, but it is likely that Samuel either wrote or supplied the information for 1:1–25:1, which covers his life and ministry until his death. The authorship of the rest of 1 Samuel cannot certainly be determined, but some suppose that Abiathar the priest wrote it.

DATE

Because of the references to the city of Ziklag, which "has belonged to the kings of Judah to this day" (27:6) and other references to Judah and Israel, we know that it was written after the division of the nation in 931 B.C. Also, since there is no mention of the fall of Samaria in 722 B.C., it should be dated before this event. The book of 1 Samuel covers a period of about 140 years, beginning with the birth of Samuel at about 1150 B.C., and ending with the death of Saul at about 1010 B.C.

WHEN THE EVENTS IN 1 & 2 SAMUEL OCCURRED

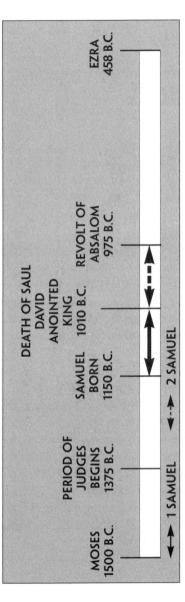

MOSES
1500 B.C.

PERIOD OF
JUDGES
BEGINS
1375 B.C.

SAMUEL
BORN
1150 B.C.

DEATH OF SAUL
DAVID
ANOINTED
KING
1010 B.C.

REVOLT OF
ABSALOM
975 B.C.

EZRA
458 B.C.

1 SAMUEL

2 SAMUEL

First Samuel shows God at work in Israel's transition...from a theocracy to an earthly kingdom. In 2 Samuel David learns to be a responsible ruler, "a man after God's own heart."

AN OUTLINE OF
1 SAMUEL

2 SAMUEL

Author:	Possibly Abiathar the Priest
Date:	Between 931 and 722 B.C.
Theme:	King David, Forerunner of the Messiah
Key Persons:	David, Nathan, Absalom, Joab, Bathsheba

AUTHOR

The two books that now make up 1 and 2 Samuel were originally one book called "The Book of Samuel." The actual author is unknown. Samuel undoubtedly had written a great deal about this time in Israel's history. However, other materials had been collected from which the actual writer could draw. Three of these are mentioned in 1 Chronicles 29:29, namely: "the book of Samuel the seer," "the book of Nathan the prophet," and "the book of Gad the seer." Both Gad and Abiathar had access to the court events of David's reign and one or both may have given us these two books.

DATE

The book has to be dated after the division of the kingdoms following Solomon's reign, 931 B.C., because of the comment in 1 Samuel 27:6, "Ziklag has belonged to the kings of Judah to this day."

THE LIFE OF
SAMUEL

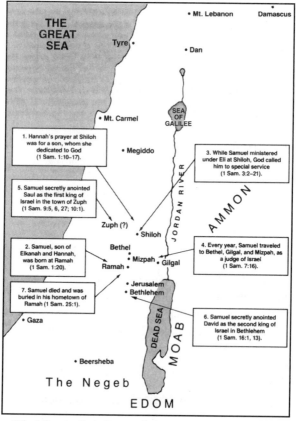

THE
GREAT
SEA

Tyre •

• Mt. Lebanon   Damascus •

• Dan

• Mt. Carmel

SEA
OF
GALILEE

• Megiddo

1. Hannah's prayer at Shiloh was for a son, whom she dedicated to God (1 Sam. 1:10–17).

3. While Samuel ministered under Eli at Shiloh, God called him to special service (1 Sam. 3:2–21).

5. Samuel secretly anointed Saul as the first king of Israel in the town of Zuph (1 Sam. 9:5, 6, 27; 10:1).

JORDAN RIVER

AMMON

Zuph (?)

• Shiloh

2. Samuel, son of Elkanah and Hannah, was born at Ramah (1 Sam. 1:20).

Bethel
•
• Mizpah
Ramah •   • Gilgal

4. Every year, Samuel traveled to Bethel, Gilgal, and Mizpah, as a judge of Israel (1 Sam. 7:16).

7. Samuel died and was buried in his hometown of Ramah (1 Sam. 25:1).

• Jerusalem
• Bethlehem

DEAD SEA

MOAB

6. Samuel secretly anointed David as the second king of Israel in Bethlehem (1 Sam. 16:1, 13).

• Gaza

• Beersheba

The Negeb

EDOM

Nelson's Complete Book of Maps and Charts © 1993, Thomas Nelson, Inc.

A_n O_utline of
SECOND SAMUEL

PART 1

THE PILLAR PRINCIPLES OF 1 AND 2 SAMUEL

JACK HAYFORD

The Pillar Principles of
1 AND 2 SAMUEL

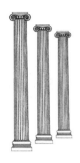

"Kingdom Life That Lasts" is a trumpet call!
It's a summons to sincerely study, then to clearly see,
the Holy Spirit's record of **three principles**, dramatically portrayed in 1 and 2 Samuel; principles which
offer us very practical assistance toward real and lasting growth in "Kingdom living." Here we can see:
- A path showing God's way to "Kingdom living";
- A perspective on God's will to enable "abiding"
  in a lifestyle of "Kingdom living."
- A pursuit—showing the way to spiritual warfare.
Here's a handbook on *walking* (forward in growth),
resting (securely) and *warring* (victoriously). These
are essential elements to "Kingdom life." What is it?

"Kingdom living" is the life Jesus wants us
all to know. In His plan, we're "born" to it. In His
promise of new birth, His own words point to *more*
than "getting saved to go to heaven." Jesus words of
"born again" promise point to "Kingdom life…
today." It is to "see" the Kingdom (i.e*., to perceive,
understand and respond*—John. 3:3); then to "enter"
it (i.e., *to become a Spirit-filled and enabled participant in service and ministry*—John 3:3, 5).

A "Kingdom life" that *lasts* will obviously be one
that not only finds salvation, but with it finds the key

15

to an *eternity* with Christ. We are seeking salvation's *present purpose*—seeking the kind of walk with Christ <u>today</u> that will bring us to a fruitfulness in life, an overcoming in spiritual warfare, and unto growing faithfulness in our love, service, and witness to others in Jesus' Name. That's what "Kingdom living" is!

A Marvelous Resource

First and Second Samuel are marvelously suited to such a purpose. In these two volumes of Old Testament history, the Holy Spirit has given us a graphic, century-long look at one of the most significant and pivotal times in the history of the children of Israel. To follow the flow of events here, is to be introduced to life-lessons that demonstrate keys to a *durable and dynamic lifestyle for New Testament believers.*

Our approach to this study is motivated by the strong prompting given in New Testament passages which point us to examine the Old Testament. These signposts direct us to expect edifying insights, not merely a historical record. For example, we are told to expect to find "**hope**" as well as "**learning**"—

> *"For whatever things were written before were written for our learning, that we through the patience and comfort of the Scriptures might have hope."*   Romans 15:4

Again, Paul urged Timothy "continue" in studying the Old Testament Scriptures, noting how they are intended to provide what is needed for a believer's healthy and complete **growth** and **equipping**—

> *"All Scripture is…profitable for doctrine, for reproof, for correction, for instruction in*

righteousness, that (the godly) may be complete,
thoroughly equipped for every good work."
2 Timothy 3:16–17

Further, Jesus emphasized the need to "search" the Old Testament scriptures to learn more about ***Him***—

"You search the Scriptures, for in them you
think you have eternal life; and these are
they which testify of Me."   John 5:39

These are only three examples, but they are explicit in their message: the New Testament emphasizes the importance of studying Old Testament history for more than mere historic interest. Rather, we are called to passages like these two books before us, because they are given for our *formation*—not simply our *in*formation!

THREE
CENTRAL PERSONALITIES

First and Second Samuel are built on a grid of three people—each one filling a central place in Israel's history.

Samuel is the bridge personality between the period of Israel's *judges* and the period of her *kings*. He is the Bible's primary "king-maker," in his anointing and introducing Israel's first two kings.

Saul is Israel's first king, and a classic study in the way a good man may be corrupted by his office. He starts well and ends miserably, and depicts the tragic potential for *losing* the "Kingdom life" God offers us.

David is Israel's second king, and he not only models the humility that characterizes a person who pleases God's heart, but also reveals the weaknesses of the flesh that can taint, tarnish, and blight that life of Kingdom triumph made available to us all.

Twelve
GREAT PRINCIPLES

Traversing the pages of 1 and 2 Samuel, **three primary themes** unfold, each opening into four subordinate ideas elaborating that theme: (1) <u>God's ways</u> leading to Kingdom living; (2) <u>God's will</u> for abiding in Kingdom living; and (3) <u>God's warfare</u>—the principles of "fighting the good fight."

GOD'S WAYS—*Leading To Kingdom Living*

Foundational to all understanding of God's ways is the fact that they so often reverse the ways of human wisdom: *"'For My thoughts are not your thoughts, nor are your ways My ways,' says the Lord"* (Isaiah 55:8). First Samuel 16:7 classically illustrates this principle in a way that offers the promise of candidacy for "Kingdom Living" to every one of us, no matter what our sense of personal limitations may be. See what God says when He selects David for that "Kingdom life" he was to fulfill. <u>His choice and call is not predicated on our apparent readiness or whether we would be the selection of human consensus.</u> *"For the Lord does not see as man sees; for man looks at the outward appearance, but the Lord looks at the heart."* That's all it takes, Child of God!

Open your heart to the possibilities of "Kingdom Living"—

- To know the **purpose** of God being fulfilled in your daily life, your family and your vocation;
- To know the **power** of God daily filling your soul to enable your praying, your service and witness.

That's Kingdom living! It is realizing the presence of King Jesus <u>flowing His rule and reign</u> into every corner of our life and experience; <u>manifesting *His* life, *His* love and *His* grace</u> through ordinary people in whom His Kingdom has come to dwell (Luke 17:21; Colossians 1:27). Here are keys to His ways:

1. **God's Heart**—*Always Opened To The Oppressed.*
   The beginning point in learning God's ways for Kingdom living is to realize *no one is outside the possibilities of heavenly royalty!* A poverty mindset and a defeatist attitude tempt us all, but the Word of God calls us to see, hear, believe and receive that <u>the possibilities of His rule *lifting us* and *advancing us*</u> are always promised; for *"He raises the poor from the dust and lifts the beggar from the ash heap, to set them among princes and make them inherit the throne of glory"* (1 Samuel 2:8).
   Those words theme Hannah's song; a woman who found the way through God's grace:

- Beyond the demeaning voice of a mocking accuser (Peninnah—like the Enemy, 1 Samuel 1:2–7)
- Beyond the wearying anguish and misunderstanding of others (1 Samuel 1:10, 14)
- Beyond barrenness and affliction, through

prayer into the peace of God (1 Samuel 1:5, 11, 17–18)

- Unto realizing the *dominion* of Kingdom victory, as the Lord *"exalts…"* (1 Samuel 2:10).

2. God's Word—*Always The Key to Life-Wisdom.*

We can never make too frequent a mention of the absolute importance of the Word of God as the key to making life work. "Wisdom" is the ability to rightly apply those principles that will effectively enable successfully dealing with all matters of daily living. Constant intake of the Bible's life, truth and food is the means for *regular refillings* with that wisdom.

First Samuel 3:1 describes a time when God's "revelation" (His Word) was not known widely. It was the era of Israel's judges—a season summarized in the words of Judges 21:25—*"everyone did what was right in his own eyes;"* a time characterized by the destructiveness of human ignorance and the wholesale ruin of human sin (example: read Judges 19–21).

The turnaround comes with Samuel. He becomes a case study in steadfast obedience to God's Word and will (1 Samuel 3:19–20), and through whom the presence of God's purpose and will are advanced because of the effect of His Word in his life (1 Samuel 3:20–21).

In contrast, it is sadly tragic to see the dismal fall of Saul's "Kingdom life" as a direct result of refusal to heed God's Word (1 Samuel 13:13–14). It's frightening to see the loss of his intended rule, *"because you have not kept what the Lord commanded you."*

3. **God's Voice**—*Always Calling Unto Possibilities.*
    All three of the central personalities of 1 and 2 Samuel are case studies in God's ability to bring the unlikely to a place of significance.

- Samuel is a mere boy, but he is visited by the Lord, hears His **voice** and answers (1 Samuel 3:10).
- Saul is a bumpkin, but he is selected by God's grace and overflowed with His **Spirit** (1 Samuel 10:6–13).
- David is a shepherd, but he is anointed and **gifted** to bring deliverance to a nation (1 Samuel l6–17).

It is the way and the delight of the Lord to call us beyond the limits of our own capacities, unto the broad dimensions of His possibilities for us. Ours is to listen—then to trust and obey, in dependence upon His leading, His Spirit, and His enabling gifts.

4. **God's Anointing**—*Always A Lifetime Gift…Until.*
    There is a peculiarity in the mercy of God; one that often puts His own reputation at risk. It is revealed in the words of Romans 11:29: *"For the gifts and calling of God are irrevocable."* In short, we find in His Word that when God makes a commitment, He never withdraws it—*even when the subject of that commitment becomes unworthy of His goodness.* It is this trait of God's mercy that explains why we will sometime see believers who are living inconsistently or in compromise, yet who still seem to be enjoying the blessing of God upon their work or ministry.

First John 2:20, 26 describe "an anointing" which abides—one which enables and instructs. The *limits* of that anointing are not specifically described, but it is apparent from Scripture that God is incredibly willing to allow the anointing upon an individual to continue to function *beyond* the place human patience would tolerate a violation of trust.

Such mercy and tolerance is usually misinterpreted by its recipient. Sometimes observers will make the same mistake—drawing the conclusion, "If God still is blessing *through* that person, everything must be all right." But it isn't true. Saul is the ultimate and most disastrous example in the Bible of a man who began with God's anointing, but who lost his place of "Kingdom" rule (1 Samuel 15:28) — and who died as one "not anointed with oil" (2 Samuel 1:21). <u>There is an amazing patience God shows toward us that *always desires* to sustain His anointing upon us. But there is an "until"…a place where insistent willfulness brings its end.</u>

GOD'S WILL—*Abiding In Kingdom Living*

The above concluding lesson about God's ways is a sobering warning. To *enter* "Kingdom Life" is not to receive a license to the flesh's interpretation of that life. Rather, it is to begin learning "to abide"—a basic principle which Jesus calls us to (read John 15), and which is graphically illustrated in 1 and 2 Samuel. Here are four concepts to embrace…and *abide* in:

5. God's Honor—*Always Guard Against Pride.*

The foremost trait of David's life is his *heart for God.* It was this quality God most sought when seeking one He could bring to Kingdom rule (1 Samuel 13:14) and it is *still* the quality He seeks to this day (2 Chronicles 16:9). When God made

David His choice, He specifically says He was looking "at the heart" (1 Samuel 16:7).

This quality is sometime supposed to indicate a level of spiritual accomplishment or unexcelled holiness, and such a presupposition tends to produce religious self-righteousness, codes and preempting attitudes toward others. But David's obvious imperfections are glaringly apparent at times, and while they are never taken lightly, neither do they block the realization of God's purpose through his life. Why?

The reason is because David always *honors* God. He is the first to worship God's greatness (see his many psalms); he is quick to humble himself in God's presence (2 Samuel 6:21–22); he is immediate to confess sin (2 Samuel 12:13); and he *constantly refuses to defend himself!* This last trait— which honors God by leaving all self-vengeance in God's hands, and never rising to assert his own self—is probably the greatest evidence of a man who honors God.

- **See it** when he refuses to elevate himself, even though multitudes sing his praise and laud his achievements (compare 2 Samuel 18:7 with 18:14, 18).
- **See it** when he refuses to retaliate; when he might have taken Saul's life and been excused in the eyes of many for doing so (1 Samuel 24:1–22).
- **See it** when he refuses to rise to his own defense when Absalom revolts against him (2 Samuel 15:13–26).
- **See it** when Shimei curses and throws stones at him at the time of his flight (2 Samuel 16:1–13).

Loved one, _this is the heart of "honoring God."_ To honor Him is not merely an emotional or intellectual act of worship, nor is it to give greatly or to serve colorfully. In the last analysis, to honor is to hold your ground of commitment and trust when everything is against you. To honor your trustworthiness on the job, even when unappreciated. To lovingly care for your spouse even when misunderstanding arises, and to stand by your marriage vows even when dark or trying days come. This is "honoring." And David provides us a great picture of this central issue that reveals the "Kingdom life" that _abides._

6. God's Presence—_Always Prioritize Worship._

It is possible that 2 Samuel, chapters 5 and 6 may provide us with the greatest picture in the Bible to that understanding _of_ and passion _for worshipping God_ which will bring the fullest fruitage to our quest for true "Kingdom living." David understood the _essence_ of God's desire regarding worship: **God wants to dwell among His people** (Exodus 25:8). He also understood that **worship is the means for welcoming God's presence** (Psalm 22:3).

No principle of "Kingdom life" is more essential to our understanding and response. Worship is not an exercise, it is a heartcry! David's longing to bring the Ark into Jerusalem was not born of a ritual idea, it was rooted in a recognition that God's presence is essential to realizing the fulfillment of my rule. The Ark was more than the _symbol_ of God's presence: His power was _present_ there, and it was manifest. So David's urgency to "bring up the Ark of God" (2 Samuel 6:2) is clearly motivated by his recognition: I cannot fulfill *my* "kingdom role" without the daily presence of *THE King!*

In this episode we confront three critical issues:

- Worship that will remain *alive* must always be pursued and sustained on God's terms. 1 Chronicles 15 fills in an important part of the story in 2 Samuel 6. David's discovery of "God's way of worship" is pivotal, and we are reminded that we are not at liberty to suppose "anything goes" in our worship. There is a reverence demanded.

- Worship allows for great rejoicing, and that joy will often require a childlike humility to release its expression. David's dancing was not meant as a "show." To remember his high office, and to see his lowliness of childlikeness is to be reminded that God delights in open expressiveness; but it needs to be motivated by humility, not in a carnal pride over one's "display" (2 Samuel 6:14–22).

- Worship which resists humility and is without a passion for God's presence begets an atmosphere of barrenness. Michal's critical spirit (2 Samuel 6:20) results in unfruitfulness. Just as there is a "death penalty" for neglecting God's order (2 Samuel 6:6–7), so there is a penalty for pride: lost intimacy, and no new life in the household.

7. **God's Faithfulness**—*Always There "In The Dark."*
The spirit of worship will lead to a steadfastness in trial—another key to "Kingdom Living That Lasts." It is important to see how David's difficulties result in his being deepened in the conviction:

God is faithful!

Read the following accounts in David's life, then read the Psalm that he wrote as a result of that experience. David learned, God is always there in life's darkest moments. Read…and see how these may apply to yours.

- 2 Samuel 16:5–14—Compare with Psalm 7.
- 2 Samuel 22—is essentially Psalm 18.
- 1 Samuel 21:10–15—Compare with Psalm 34.
- 2 Samuel 11, 12—Compare with Psalm 51.
- 1 Samuel 22—Compare with Psalm 52.
- 1 Samuel 23—Compare with Psalm 54, 142.
- 1 Samuel 24—Compare with Psalm 57.
- 1 Samuel 19—Compare with Psalm 59.
- 2 Samuel 8—Compare with Psalm 60.
- 1 Samuel 22:5—Compare with Psalm 63.

It is impossible to read the setting of these songs without noticing two outstanding facts: (1) David's greatest songs are written at the time of his greatest struggles; (2) David's darkest times are the moments when the light of God's faithfulness shined the brightest. Let these facts undergird your "Kingdom life."

8. God's Sovereignty—*Always Working His Will.*

An amazing evidence of God's ability to use frail human vessels—to achieve His purpose *through* and *beyond* our limitations—is demonstrated in remarkable ways in 1 and 2 Samuel. Perhaps one of the most fascinating cases of this is seen in an apparent paradox.

To begin, when the people ask for a king, the Lord makes clear that this is not His *first* plan (1 Samuel 8:5–7).

Still, He leads Samuel to Saul and directs him to anoint him (1 Samuel 9:15–16); then, God's Word explains that God would have established Saul's kingdom over Israel "forever" (1 Samuel 13:13) except for the fact that Saul violated the terms of God's covenant. <u>*In other words,*</u> God was fully committed to Saul: His term of duty was not a "pretend time," simply tolerated by God in order to get to "the real thing" when David appears.

The point of noticing these biblical facts is that they reveal to us the marvel of God's magnificent mix of wisdom and mercy, manifest in His steadfast movement toward the achieving of His will.

- He knows the end from the beginning...yet, he never "plays with human destiny" as though we were disposable, dispensable chess pieces. (See God's heart in David's lament—2 Samuel 12:17–27.)
- He makes a solid—indeed, eternal—commitment to those He invites to "Kingdom life," even though he knows they will later revoke their trust. (Note all God did to help secure Saul's kingdom: 1 Samuel 10:10, 26; 11:6, 13–15; 12:13; 13:13.)
- He continues to justly achieve His purpose, even though the failures of those He uses would preempt their place, *if they rely on His mercy rather than their righteousness—they receive the Kingdom...FOREVER!* (2 Samuel 7:1–29)

GOD'S WAR—*Fighting The Good Fight*
All New Testament teaching reveals that maturity will bring us to an abiding <u>peace</u> *within* our

hearts, but to relentless spiritual <u>warfare</u> our *whole lifetime*. (a) Jesus' call to discipleship includes a call to measure the cost of battle (Luke 14:25–33). (b) Ephesians 1–6 reveals the progress and process of growth leads "finally" to spiritual warfare (Ephesians 6:10–20). Look at these Old Testament stories to gain insight for New Testament warfare:

9. God's Passion—*Always Calling to Boldness.*

Two episodes in these books of Samuel remind us of the need for passion and boldness in spiritual warfare. Saul's fury over the merciless and cruel negotiation offered by Nahash the Ammonite is stirring to behold (1 Samuel 11:1–7). David's indignation over the arrogant pratings of Goliath, as he defies the Name of the Lord God of Israel is equally instructive (1 Samuel 17:26–31). Applied today, we are reminded it is fundamental to prayer warfare that if there is no passion, little will be accomplished—indeed, little will be attempted!

James 5:16 teaches that for prayer to "avail much" in our day, it must be "effective" (that is, energized by the Holy Spirit) and "fervent" (that is, impassioned with human concern). Emotionless prayer is as undesirable as faithless prayer. <u>True faith</u> *stirs the soul*: <u>true passion</u> *stands on God's Word.*

10. God's Resources—*Always Ready to Refresh.*

First Samuel 14 contain an insight into our need for spiritual refreshing in battle. Jonathan's faith and pursuit bring him to draw on a resource that had been (without his knowledge) prohibited by his father. At this time, Saul is becoming a small-souled, jealous, self-centered wimp—a giant of a man, so preoccupied with himself he has lost perspective of God's people and their need. His only concern is his vindication, not the victory of his people.

The analogy is too tempting to fail to note: Jonathan depicts a generation that is winning in battle because it is drawing on a divinely provided resource that is both *sweet* and *strengthening*. Another generation speaks prohibition against such partaking—but in the end, the righteousness of the issue becomes manifest: *"(Jonathan) has worked with God this day!"* (1 Samuel 14:45). May God keep us humble…drawing on His resources of power through praise, worship and Spirit-filled living and prayer. Some may forbid them—but they are the keys to refreshing in battle.

11. God's Direction—*Always Ready To Be Known.*
Nothing is more essential to "Kingdom Living" than humbly depending upon God's direction for our life. *"Trust in the Lord with all your heart, and lean not on your own understanding; in all your ways acknowledge Him, and He shall direct your paths"* (Proverbs 3:5–6). There are numerous cases of God's leading when David seeks His guidance. Read 1 Samuel 16 to 1 Kings 2—covering his lifetime—and note all the instances David "inquired of the Lord" (e.g. 2 Samuel 5:19, 23) or in other ways seeks and accepts divine direction. God still answers such a quest.

12. God's Mercy—*Available For Fallen Warriors.*
We dare not leave this study without noting one

last and crucial issue of "Kingdom living": *There are sometime severe casualties in the battle.* People "fall" in many ways, but none seems more damaging than when a moral failure like David's mars the slate of a good soldier-leader. Leaders succumb to sickness, to doubts and fear, to intimidation, and to other failures. If any lessons are to be underscored for us as we pursue the spiritual warfare today, let these be fixed in mind: (1) Never vaunt your own holiness, or boast over your superior standard (Galatians 6:1c, 3; 1 Corinthians 10:12). (2) Let the mercy of God prevail in every possible case: God loves mercy even more than justice (Micah 7:18–20). (3) Always seek to restore fallen leaders (Galatians 6:1a). This does not mean to instantly return them to duty. It means to require the extended time needed to minister to their recovery, and to see in them the re-establishment of proven patterns of godly leadership which the Word requires (1 Timothy 3:1–13).

And so, FORWARD…to possess the possibilities!

Principle #1 focused God's ability to lift us beyond our limits—principle #12, our need to always remember that mercy; showing it to others. And thus, we conclude.

Now, dear friend, take Samuel's message with you into your tomorrows. The privilege and the possibilities of "ruling in Christ and under Christ" are ours. As ones saved and called to *His* Kingdom in this day, His *charge* is our *chance*—our chance to become "kings" whose "rule" _lasts_—through Him!

PART 2

THE RELEVANT ANSWERS IN 1 AND 2 SAMUEL

SCOTT BAUER

1 AND 2 SAMUEL

These books represent a kind of high water mark in the Bible for the way people use religious superstition in an attempt to influence the world around them. This religious superstition is reflected in such seemingly mundane ways as an inattention to the parenting responsibilities of spiritual leaders, who believe that maintaining the forms of religious observance substitute for true spiritual leadership. This superstition is also witnessed in the use of religious implements such as "good luck" charms in battle and in substituting sacramental observances for faith and obedience.

The limited human worldview revealed in a thorough study of this book, concerning our tendency to try and influence God through external measures, is not simply found in the ancient world of Samuel, Saul, and David. It is a continuing presence in our world today. The same fears which drove the ancients to attempt to summon spiritual powers at times of profound need are still present today. And our response to them can be as confused and destructive as witnessed in these books.

There are other sets of problems in the books of Samuel that are related to the profound and complex moral and metaphysical questions about our world. First Samuel has been used as a banner text for the sanctifying of homosexual relationships. It has been wrongly claimed that David and Jonathan represent such a pairing. The perversion of our own culture has not allowed us to evaluate basic human relationships without the presumed addition of sexual disobedience and deviation. There is yet another set of questions in these books related to the occult practices of necromancy and receiving instructions for living from the dead. The occultic attempt to summon the dead is displayed in Saul's desperate action to understand his own future. It opens the way for serious questions to the nature of the spirit world, reincarnation, and the place of the dead and the relationship of the living to this world.

Superstition in the Lives of God's People

Superstition results from the misguided notion that human religious forms can influence God to do the things that are highest on the human agenda. It is directly related to the separation of our responsibility to respond to God according to His revealed will and to substitute for that the exercise of religious rituals. It can be seen in families and nations. In the books of Samuel, it underscores disastrous consequences in personal tragedies which result from spiritual activity apart from a vital and personal relationship with God.

Parenting Problems in 1 & 2 Samuel

Eli the Judge, Samuel the Prophet, and David the King all failed the test of bringing the next generation—their own children—to a point of faithful pursuit in the things of God and to fruitful living as those who walk with Him in integrity. In the midst of God's presence and with a supernatural witness to the reality of God's power, the inability of these parents to communicate their own faith to their children stands as a stark testimony to parents of all generations for the need of making the love of God a first-hand experience for their children.

"Now the sons of Eli were corrupt…" (1 Samuel 2:12). Eli served as the judge over Israel for forty years; the text says that he was both blind and obese (4:15–18). This reference to Eli is clearly a physical one, but it offers insight to the broader spiritual nature of the indulgence he showed as a father.

The presence of spiritual mission in the absence of practical disciplines always brings destruction to the families of spiritual leaders—in fact the same is true in any believing family. Eli conducted his spiritual ministry adequately to the people of Israel, but the indictment that his sons *"did not know the Lord" (2:12)* stands as a monument to all parents who attend to their spiritual needs and those of others, but not to those of the people closest to them.

The pattern of indulgence of Eli's sons has remarkably familiar patterns to it that are universal in all generations. We mistakenly tend to ascribe the sins of our day to the heightened corruption of the times, when, in fact, it is merely the reflection of unredeemed humanity in any generation.

Eli's sons took for themselves the offerings which rightly belonged to the Lord (2:14–17). Their impatience to wait for the sacrifice to be completed, so that they could appropriately claim their portion, constituted a robbery of the offering of God. The brutish intimidation of worshipers was another aspect of the sins of Hophni and Phineas. And it was their most grievous sin before God: *"The sin of the young men was very great before the Lord, for men **abhorred the offering of the Lord**"* (2:17).

They also used their priestly roles to sexually exploit women who came to worship (2:22). The condemnation which came to Eli from *"a man of God"* (2:27), results in a death sentence for the boys and Eli himself. But the critical matter in challenging Eli is succinctly stated 2:29—Eli honors his sons more than the Lord. And in so doing, he guarantees their destruction and brings dishonor to his own leadership.

First Samuel describes Eli's displeasure with the actions of his sons—but he never rises to remove them from the office of spiritual leadership which they violated, and he never accepts the responsibility before God to rectify the situation. His complaints are hollowed by his own blindness and personal indulgence. His obesity at a physical dimension has slowed his responses to the Lord, and his physical blindness is matched by a spiritual confusion which is profound. Though Eli sees their sin—he sees no way to correct or punish it. This is not merely the fault of any old man who has lost his strength, but it is the pattern of a father who has indulged his children over a lifetime.

The judgment of God against the boys is the most graphic illustration of the price of parental indulgence (2:30–34; 4:11–18). It ultimately leads to death.

The pattern of parental indulgence continues with Samuel himself. Having lived in the house of Eli and having experienced his first supernatural encounter with God (a word of condemnation to Eli over the abuses of his sons—3:11–14), it would have seemed natural that Samuel would not have repeated Eli's mistakes with his own sons. However, that was not the case.

Samuel's sons were dishonest, corrupt, and used their spiritual influence in a way that benefited them personally at the expense of a righteous application of their office in serving the needs of God's people (1 Samuel 8:1–6). It was this absence of integrity in Samuel's sons (Joel and Abijah) which directly impacted the future of Israel. *"Then all the elders of Israel gathered together and came to Samuel at Ramah, and said to him, 'Look, you are old, and your sons do not walk in your ways. Now make us a king to judge us like all the nations'"* (8:4–5). The issue of Israel's desire for a king may never have occurred if Samuel had been more discerning with his sons.

How is it possible that Samuel would even consider making his sons judges over Israel when it was so obvious that they lacked the moral and spiritual character to carry out such an assignment? The pattern of this kind of parental blindness is nothing new to our generation! It is a reflection of the hopes of parents for their children being realized without the enormous price of parenting God's way that is enforced over a lifetime.

David's sons reflect some of the same patterns of indulgence witnessed in the lives of Israel's last two judges. David's son, Amnon, raped his own half-sister (2 Samuel 13). As a result, Absalom murdered Amnon, his brother. The wicked violence in David's own home is part of the spiritual consequence of David's sin with Bathsheba and the eventual murder of her husband, Uriah.

The wickedness of David's sons is not limited to this one incident. Two of David's sons (Absalom and Adonijah) led rebellions against their father, claiming the throne of Israel for themselves. The death of Absalom marked the deepest sorrow of David's life (2 Samuel 18:33). The later rebellion of Adonijah (in 1 Kings) pitted brother against brother and insured a heritage of pain. However, there is a vital insight into the process of parenting which pulls back the curtain on David and his family. *"And his father had not rebuked him at any time by saying, 'Why have you done so?' He was also a very good-looking man"* (1 Kings 1:6). Adonijah was Absalom's younger brother by the same mother. The question remains open as to whether David's own parenting practices guaranteed the rebellion which later threatened his kingdom and brought about the destruction of the boys he loved.

In all three cases (Eli, Samuel, David), these were men who knew and loved God and yet, they were unable to communicate that love to their sons. There is a superstitious notion among the people of God that simply bringing your children up in a God-honoring environment will affect the kind of spiritual transformation necessary for a changed life. Nothing could be more false.

The instruction of the book of Proverbs offers

direct insight into the task of parenting. Five times in the book, "the rod" of correction is offered to parents as the way to assisting a child in understanding his/her place in the world. Foolishness, death, and destruction are replaced by the rod of correction with faithfulness, humility, and life. *"The **rod and rebuke give wisdom**, but a child left to himself brings shame to his mother"* (Proverbs 29:15). It is very likely that this parable was first framed around the witness of David's own royal family. Solomon's (David's son by Bathsheba) comments make perfect sense in the light of his own experience concerning the lives of his half brothers Amnon, Absalom, and Adonijah.

The diligence with which we pursue our spiritual life must be conveyed to the next generation. It is not mystically conveyed through religious observances or forms. Sacramental participation, church attendance, and concerns for the things of God do not guarantee a personal transformation of character and spirit in the next generation. It is the dutiful prayer, consistent discipline, continual confrontation with spiritual growth, and the unwavering commitment to shape both the patterns of behavior and the attitudes which surround that behavior that are the only means for securing the next generation of the people of God.

The Ark of the Covenant

The elders of Israel summoned the ark of the covenant to go before them in battle in 1 Samuel 4:3. In partnership with Eli's sons, the ark was brought before the army of Israel and preceded them in battle.

"When the ark of the covenant of the Lord came

into the camp, all Israel shouted so loudly that the earth shook" (4:5). The ark was the single most holy representation of the presence of God in Israel. It is described in Exodus 25:10–22 as a beautiful wooden box overlaid with gold. It carried the testimony of God's faithful witness to Israel. Above the ark, the mercy seat was fashioned to receive the sacrifice for the sins of the people.

The roar of the army at the presence of the ark is troubling for two reasons. First—the unbelieving, sinful priests (Eli's sons—Hophni and Phineas) were leading the way. Second—the people were not calling on God, but rather cheering the symbols of His presence. This is not unlike carrying a rabbit's foot in your pocket for good luck. The ark was not a good luck charm. And God would not honor the presentation of the ark as a rallying point for war. He—Himself—is the object of Israel's faith and nothing else.

The result of the battle verifies God's disapproval—Israel was defeated and the ark lost to the enemies of Israel. However, once they captured the ark, all of 1 Samuel 5 and 6 then describe the process of how the Philistines try to rid themselves of its presence. It proved to be a curse in their temple (the statue of Dagon was mysteriously toppled and destroyed), and the land of the Philistines was overrun with vermin, plagues, and problems until the ark was returned to Israel.

Sacrifice and Superstition

Saul, Israel's king, faced an overwhelming challenge early in his rule when he was threatened by an enormous Philistine army in 1 Samuel 13. His response to this produced the first recorded failure in his leadership. Because of his impatience and his fear, Saul acted unwisely and opened the way to a process which eventually cost him his leadership and his life.

Saul was told to wait one week for Samuel to come and then sacrifice would be offered before they went into battle. However, Saul recognized the lagging morale of his troops and the need to act—so he took upon himself the responsibilities of the spiritual leadership of the people. Immediately upon Saul's presumption in offering the sacrifice, Samuel entered and pronounced a harsh sentence: *"You have done foolishly. You have not kept the commandment of the Lord your God, which He commanded you. For now the Lord would have established your kingdom over Israel forever. But now your kingdom shall not continue…"* (1 Samuel 13:13–14).

It is the use of sacrifice as a means of utilitarian crowd manipulation that expresses fear and doubt, rather than the presentation of sacrifice as an act of worship conducted in faith and obedience which constitutes Saul's failure. It is this same notion of religious action, conducted merely to advance our human agenda on our own terms, which misses the point of a faith-filled, obedient walk with God.

This is further illustrated in the second of Saul's failures in leadership. In 1 Samuel 15:3, the prophet instructed Saul to *"utterly destroy all that they have, and do not spare them. But kill man and woman, infant and nursing child, ox and sheep, camel and donkey."* This is a punishment imposed on the

Amalekites for their treachery toward Israel.

Saul's response in sparing the king and some of the livestock had nothing to do with mercy or spiritual devotion. When Samuel confronted him, Saul hid behind his answer that this was done due to his devotion to God through his intended sacrifice of the animals. Samuel's searing rebuke in the power of the Spirit of God forever answered the question of disobedience to the revealed will of God based on a presumption of good religious intent. ***"To obey is better than sacrifice…for rebellion is as the sin of witchcraft, and stubbornness is as iniquity and idolatry…"*** (1 Samuel 15:22–23). God is not at all interested in the nuance of our additions to His commandments or our creative interpretation of them.

Saul's disobedience and pride-filled response to the commandment of God mocked the Lord and revealed the corrupted core of a man who used to walk humbly with God. *"When you were little in your own eyes, were you not head of the tribes of Israel? And did not the Lord anoint you king over Israel?"* (1 Samuel 15:17). Saul's sin and his attempts to cover it with religious action undermined the very foundation of his leadership.

It is the separation of faith and obedience from the pursuit of God which consistently leads people to confusion, disobedience, and idolatry in their spiritual life.

Even the most sincere efforts at spiritual pursuit can lead to superstition when those who come to God are driven by fears and are moved to offer forms of religious action that are devoid of faith. Our response to the Lord must be consistent with what has been revealed to us in His Word, and it must be offered from a heart of faith.

This is probably best illustrated in the New Testament in Mark 16:16, *"He who believes and is baptized will be saved; but he who does not believe will be condemned."* The Lord links faith with the action of baptism in this passage. However, baptism without faith is meaningless, and there is condemnation for those who refuse faith. The mere expressions of spiritual action (baptism, communion) do not in themselves represent an adequate response to God without the faith of the individual which ascribes value and meaning to them. God is not interested in religious actions; He is interested in our obedience to Him (1 Samuel 15:22).

Reincarnation and Necromancy
(1 Samuel 28:3–25)

There is a continual twist in the human experience which seeks to discover information from spiritual sources wherever possible. The Holy Spirit offers a complete array of gifts for this very purpose —1 Corinthians 12:8–12. Wisdom, knowledge, prophecy, and discernment of spirits are all available to the people of God as they function in the supernatural gifts of the Holy Spirit. These gifts are available to all who have been baptized with the Holy Spirit (Acts 1:5). The Lord is not distant, nor is He mysterious about our understanding the spiritual challenges we confront in our day-to-day living. He is available and desirous that we be equipped for every good work (2 Timothy 3:17). Therefore, He has given us His Word and, because of His love for the Body of Christ and His desire for ministry to all people, He has given the gifts of the Holy Spirit (1 Corinthians 12). However, the sinful heart of man is not satisfied with this abundant resource from heaven.

Saul illustrated this in his pursuit of the prophet Samuel after his death. Saul's desperate attempts to know the future led him to a witch who he asked to conjure up the dead prophet. This pathetic attempt to know the future is the final chapter in Saul's free-fall from his leadership position as king of Israel.

In 1 Samuel 28:6, Saul consulted the Lord, but "*the Lord did not answer him, either by dreams or by Urim or by the prophets.*" These were legitimate means by which God instructed His people. We understand how God can use our dreams or the prophets to speak to us. We are more unfamiliar with the "Urim." Exodus 28:29–30 describes the Urim as being placed on the breastplate of the high priest and used for judgment in consulting the way of the Lord for leading the people of Israel.

The sinful and disobedient Saul had so compromised his walk with God that his pursuit of knowledge was not based in his desire to serve God or His people (the only reason the Lord offers the gifts of the Holy Spirit in the first place), but because he was consumed with his own fears and desperate in his personal situation. This myopic, self-centered pursuit of God was unrewarded. And in complete disobedience to his own charge as king (1 Samuel 28:3), Saul sought a necromancer to summon the dead Samuel.

The Bible is excruciatingly specific about the matter of communicating with the dead: "You shall not permit a sorceress to live" (Exodus 22:18); *"Give no regard to mediums and familiar spirits; do not seek after them, to be defiled by them"* (Leviticus 19:31); *"A man or a woman who is a medium, or who has familiar spirits, shall surely be put to death"* (Leviticus 20:27); **"There shall not be found among you anyone who makes his son or his daughter pass through the fire, or one who practices witchcraft, or a soothsayer, or one who interprets omens, or a sorcerer, or one who conjures spells, or a medium, or a spiritist, or one who calls up the dead"** (Deuteronomy 18:10–11).

The detailed rejection of these practices is related to the spirit through which they are conducted. The pursuit of knowledge on this basis opens the individual to the demonic realm and all of the perversions, idolatries, and hellish destruction which comes as a result. The seductive ways of the devil never cease to draw the curious, the naive, and the rebellious to their own destruction. The very real information offered by the demons, who traffic in the perversions listed above, is "tainted" and leads the person deeper into confusion and farther from God. The Bible teaches that the devil is a liar and the source of all lies (John 8:44). From the garden of Eden, the pursuit of "knowledge" outside of the expressed purpose to serve God and to minister to people proves to be the way of vanity and destruction.

The occultic practices outlawed in the Old Testament apply in our own times. The destructive power of these practices continues to destroy people today. The pursuit of a "New Age" revelation of spiritual power which rejects the one true and living God and His Word, as revealed in the Bible, leads people to a dead end, as witnessed by Saul's own suicide and the destruction of his family (1 Samuel 31:2–4).

The issue of reincarnation is also called into question by this text. Hebrews 9:27, *"It is appointed for men to die once, but after this the judgment."* Second Corinthians 5:8–11 clearly teaches that death leads us into the presence of God and that we are judged by Jesus Christ. Jesus describes a chasm between the living and the dead which cannot be crossed (Luke 16:26). The idea that man has endless successions of opportunities to get life right and start over again is false. Man only gets one chance at life. But there is hope! Jesus is very clear about this: ***"You must be born again"*** (John 3:7). **This is a spiritual rebirth based in faith in Jesus Christ.** All the talk about reincarnation is a matter of lying spirits deceiving people in order to lead them to their final destruction.

Homosexuality (2 Samuel 1:26)

For those committed to a social reinterpretation of the Bible, this text is the banner for homosexuality: *"I am distressed for you, my brother Jonathan; you have been very pleasant to me; your love to me was wonderful, surpassing the love of women."* The obvious intent of the text is to assert the deep distress David experienced upon hearing of Jonathan's death in battle at Mount Gilboa (1 Samuel 31:1–3). They were related through family as Jonathan was Saul's son and David was Saul's son-in-law. They had fought together for years in battle. They had served the king together with faithfulness. And Jonathan was a faithful friend to David who recognized the anointing of God upon his life, even to the extent of rejecting his own right of succession to the throne of Israel in David's behalf (1 Samuel 20:31).

"The soul of Jonathan was knit to the soul of David, and Jonathan loved him as his own soul" (1 Samuel 18:1). Clearly, the record of David's many wives and children does not suggest that David had any deficiency of interest in sexual relations with women. In fact, the single greatest failure of David's life involved his adultery with Bathsheba which provided the backdrop of the murder of her husband, Uriah the Hittite (2 Samuel 11). The addition by any who would suggest that David and Jonathan's relationship was anything less than completely honoring to God and within the approved guidelines of Scripture, is completely without merit.

The fact that the perversion of our time cannot fathom a relationship of meaning and substance without sexual involvement is a testimony to how far from a real understanding of love we have come. The Bible, in the New Testament, uses the English word "love" to translate three very different Greek words with completely separate ideas. The first Greek word is αγαπαω. This word describes God's perfect love for us: *"For God so **loved** the world…"* *(John 3:16)*. The second word is φιλεω. This word is used for brotherly love and it is the love of family: *"He who **loves** father and mother…"* (Matthew 10:37). This word is also used in one form for the word **kiss** as shown in Mark 14:44 and again in the Septuagint: *"Then his father Isaac said to him, 'Come near now and kiss me, my son'"* (Genesis 27:26). The Middle Eastern culture allowed for an expression of kiss which was an indication of affection apart from any sexual context. This is the same word referenced in 1 Samuel 20:41. The third word used in Greek for love is ερωσ. This relates to a sexual love between a man and a woman. The Septuagint translates Proverbs 7:18 with this kind of physical expression of love.

The kind of love described by the Septuagint in 2 Samuel 1:26 is αγαπαω—this is the kind of love that is a spiritual gift from God. David compares the depth of the spiritual partnership of his friend Jonathan as being greater than any kind of similar spiritual partnership he had known with any woman. There can be no construing of this relationship as sexual in any possible way.

The Bible is clear on the issue of homosexuality. It is forbidden and destructive to the individual and the society in which it occurs. First Corinthians 6:9 declares that homosexuals cannot enter the kingdom of heaven. Leviticus 18:22 declares homosexuality as an "abomination" before God. Leviticus 20:13 demands the death penalty for homosexuals. And Romans 1:26–27 identifies as reasons for wrath (vs. 18) the same-sex physical relationships of either men or women.

There is a temptation to single homosexuality out as being the worst of all sins—it is not. It is simply one of the things which violates God's intent for the human personality and, as a result, brings upon the person a sentence of death—as all sin does for every person. First Corinthians 6:9 clearly links all sexual immorality and perversions as preventing people from inheriting the kingdom of God. But also mentioned in the list are thieves, drunkards, revilers and extortioners (vs. 10). The reality is that homosexuality is sin. And sin—all sin—destroys people. The beauty of 1 Corinthians 6:11 is that it offers help to anyone who seeks the Lord: ***And such were some of you. But you were washed, but you were sanctified, but you were justified in the name of the Lord Jesus and by the Spirit of our God.*** We have been called out of the world and the lifestyle of our sin, so that we can be His. As we receive forgiveness and freedom from our past, God's healing and restoration can come to any person locked in sin—even the sin of homosexuality.

Conclusion

The primary source of the problems observed in these books relates to a fundamental misunderstanding of the spiritual nature of the world around us. It is not that the characters of 1 and 2 Samuel do not believe in the supernatural—it is they believe the supernatural can either be by-passed in the human experience (as in the failure of parents), or that the spiritual world around us can be manipulated by man to serve the fearful, rebellious, or ignorant whims of man.

The overwhelming message of 1 and 2 Samuel demands a humility related to our call to be people who live in a supernatural relationship with God. He is our Father—not a good luck charm. He is our Master—and we His servants. Our resource in the spiritual realm is not to do our own will, but that we be fully equipped to do **HIS WILL**. When those issues are held in clear contrast, man no longer relates to God as a superstitious force to be manipulated, but as the Lord who calls us to serve His Kingdom.

PART 3

PRACTICAL WISDOM FROM 1 AND 2 SAMUEL

JACK HAMILTON

Our God
REIGNS

Who doesn't admire heroes? They captivate our enthusiasm by their daring exploits. Our imagination is unfettered as we vicariously experience with them their victories against all odds.

These heroic personalities become points of encouragement when we are faced with overwhelming circumstances. Heroes sow in our minds a "can do" attitude. Their deeds inspire courage and fortitude in the average person.

Heroes also inspire proverbs of encouragement. The locker room where football players dress and prepare for the game is often filled with sayings that are meant to stir the emotions. One that is brought to mind is, *When the going gets tough, the tough get going.* These words are meant to become a reference point when it looks as though all is lost. The message conveyed is usually illustrated by someone who was able to extract victory from the jaws of defeat.

Such is the historic record of First and Second Samuel. It is as children that many of us were exposed to the action stories of these Bible books. Our introduction to the events and personalities of these two Old Testament books seeded in our souls the idea that if a person gave to God the whole of their being, then God would do amazing things with them.

David becomes a hero after slaying the giant long before he becomes a king. Samuel is a hero for his complete yielding to God before he becomes an honored prophet.

One wonders if it were not his memory of the deeds recorded in the Samuel writings that may have prompted Daniel to write, *The people who know their God shall be strong, and carry out great exploits* (Daniel 11:32b).

While these stories may motivate us during times of personal struggle, it is the principles that emerge that we are urged to embrace. It is the lessons learned from these biblical champions that will stifle cowardice when we are faced with contrasting moral issues.

These two books are packaged in the section of the Bible called Old Testament Books of History, but their purpose is far more than to record the history of the children of Israel. They illustrate again and again several fundamental concepts about God that are as needed now as then.

First, God is always in control and superintends human affairs to accomplish His purpose. **Second**, God's actions are calculated for the highest good of His people. **Third**, God hand-picks appropriate leaders to move His plan along. **Fourth**, God never abandons His people—He is always near. **Finally**, God is righteous and works with His people that they might reflect His character through acts of obedience.

All of these truths are woven into the fabric of the events of 1 and 2 Samuel. Their presence is not

only to incite courage but also to promote hope—
no matter how things may be stacked against us.

The record begins with a barren woman desperately seeking God and who sings a song of praise for His action of grace and blessing because of her supplication. It ends with David the king buying the threshing floor of one of his subjects to build an altar of worship on the future site of the temple. And in between are numerous episodes of failure and victory.

Our walk with God is similar to this. We begin as barren and lifeless individuals who call out for God's salvation in Jesus, and upon receiving His life we sing the Song of the Lord. Our destiny is to be a temple of God. And our King builds an eternal altar of worship in our souls. In between there are ups and downs.

How we navigate the ups and downs will determine whether we are heroes or cowards. How do you differentiate between the two? Not by an isolated time of triumph but by daily yielding to God's purpose no matter what each day may present. That is truly living HEROICALLY!

Learning the Song of Praise

The story of Hannah, the mother of Samuel, is spell-binding and wrought with emotion. No writer of fiction could imagine such a plot nor weave such a story to tug at the heart of a reader.

Hannah's marriage to Elkanah is filled with love. There was one element in this union, however, that tormented her soul. She was childless.

The declaration that in marriage *two shall*

become one flesh (Ephesians 5:31) is not just a statement regarding physical intimacy, but implied too is a promise that as a result of the sexual union a child would be born. The contribution of each of the pair would be realized in another life—the two fully being expressed in the one.

It was this implied promise that had not been fulfilled in her marriage. Elkanah's love for Hannah was deep and sincere regardless that as a couple they were childless. Her barrenness weighed so heavy on her soul that even her husband's reassurance of his devotion could not ease her sorrow, *Am I not better to you than ten sons?* (1 Samuel 1:8b).

Compounding her dilemma was that others viewed her childless state as a testimony that God had abandoned her. One can only imagine the sense of inadequacy she felt. This is more than enough to cause her to become isolated and bitter.

Instead she goes with the family unit to worship God and covenants with Him that if He would give her a son, she in turn would give back to Him that which meant most to her—the very son she longed for (1 Samuel 1:11). The answer she received, *Go in peace, and the God of Israel grant your petition which you have asked of Him* (1 Samuel 1:17), contained both a promise and an insight into God's purpose for providing a future leader for the nation.

Sometime later she returns to Shiloh with the child Samuel (Hebrew, *Shemu'el*, "Heard by God") and leaves him with the priest Eli to be nurtured in the service of the Lord. In so doing she fulfills her vow and the Lord blesses her with five more children (1 Samuel 2:21).

At the presentation of Samuel, Hannah breaks forth in a song of praise (1 Samuel 2:1–10). The words of her psalm celebrate these unalterable truths: God is powerful and holy (vv. 1, 2), God silences the critics of His people (v. 3), God reverses circumstances (vv. 4–8), God provides for His people (v. 9), and God defeats His adversaries and exalts the anointed King (v. 10).

This song is the precursor of another song, by another woman (Mary), who releases her firstborn son (Jesus) to God for the purpose of the redemption of humanity (Luke 1:46–55), for Jesus is the anointed King Eternal (Revelation 19:11–16).

This story is analogous to our own. We were spiritually lifeless and barren because of sin (Ephesians 2:1). Upon crying out to God for His salvation, we come alive spiritually through the new birth (John 3:3, 5–8). As a result of this marvelous miracle, we break forth in the song of the saved—

I waited patiently for the LORD;
And He inclined to me,
And heard my cry.
He also brought me up out of a
horrible pit,
Out of the miry clay,
And set my feet upon a rock,
And established my steps.
He has put a new song in my mouth—
Praise to our God;
Many will see it and fear,
And will trust in the LORD.
(Psalm 40:1–3)

Learning to Stand for God

Nobody likes whiners. Listening to their constant lament is as irritating as scratching on a blackboard. Their cries that life is too hard or there is no support for them soon wearies even the most patient of people. We have to face the fact that there is no perfect situation or environment on the earth. Therefore, we need to hitch up our pants and set our faces to the wind. The Apostle Paul put it this way—*having done all, to stand. Stand therefore...* (Ephesians 6:13, 14).

Samuel seemed to be placed in an ideal situation. He would live at Shiloh, the central place of worship for Israel. He would be mentored by the priest/judge Eli in the ways of the Lord.

In reality, however, all was not well. Eli's sons, who were priests at the tabernacle, were corrupt, greedy, and sensual (1 Samuel 2:12–17, 22). The ark of the covenant was taken from its place and was held in the hands of Israel's enemies at another site for a prolonged period of time (1 Samuel 4:3–7:2). Idolatry was practiced throughout the land (1 Samuel 7:3–4). And even Samuel's sons who became judges were dishonest, probably the result of what had become the practice of other judges throughout the land (1 Samuel 8:2–3). Perhaps the most chilling fact about this time is found in these words written in 1 Samuel 3:1, *And the word of the LORD was rare in those days; there was no widespread revelation.*

In spite of these conditions, Samuel develops into a man of God (1 Samuel 2:21, 26). As a youth he learns to acknowledge the voice of God (1 Samuel 3:4–10), and to speak His word with courage and clarity (1 Samuel 3:19). As a result he spearheads a revival which overthrows the worship of idols (1 Samuel 7:2–6) and intercedes for Israel as they fight their notorious enemy the Philistines. Samuel's efforts bring about the victory and is memorialized with a stone called the *Ebenezer*, meaning *the LORD has helped us* (1 Samuel 7:10–14).

As the judge of Israel he traveled around the countryside speaking the word of the Lord and leading the people in the worship of God. He also established an altar of worship in his hometown of Ramah where he always returned to minister to those who came to him (7:15–17).

When Samuel aged, he faced a challenge that was unthinkable to him. Because of the corruption of his own sons the people came to him asking for a king. The Bible records that this idea displeased him, but rather than debating he prayed and to his surprise God granted the people their desire. The Lord told Samuel to say that this change would have consequences that would be hard and harsh. Nevertheless, Israel was determined to have a king, and God told Samuel to heed to their wish.

The record reports Samuel anointed two men as king of Israel—Saul, the people's choice and David, God's choice. Even with a king Samuel remains the conscience of the people and warns them to follow the Lord and not to forsake His ways. He lives long enough to see the failure of Saul and the beginning of the ascendancy of David.

Samuel is a wonderful model for people to mimic. His entire life was lived with integrity. He was committed to God and His people. Samuel's life still speaks eloquently to those who will serve the Lord today.

Upon committing our lives to God through Christ, like Samuel we should sensitize our hearts to the Spirit of God and live in the dynamic of His word to us. This prophet of God lived with courage in the face of various forms of pressure to compromise. He did not compromise and neither should we.

Learning the Importance of Finishing Well

The old children's story of the tortoise and the hare is applicable when one looks at the life of Saul. Remember how when the race between the two began, the hare sped off and distanced himself from the plodding tortoise. It looked as though this was a laughable contest. At the finish however, the tortoise wins because he just kept moving forward. The hare on the other hand, because he started so well and had a large lead, pulled off the course and fell asleep thereby losing the race.

No one in all of Israel had more potential than Saul the son of Kish. His father was wealthy and had a good reputation. Saul himself was physically attractive and a trusted son with a sense of humility (1 Samuel 9:1–3).

On a mission to retrieve some of his father's livestock, he seeks out the prophet Samuel. God had prepared Samuel for the visit by telling him of Saul's coming. And in obedience to God's command, when the two get together the prophet anoints Saul as king, the *commander over His* (the Lord's*) inheritance* (1 Samuel 10:1).

At first Saul seems to be an excellent choice. The Spirit of the Lord comes upon him and he begins to prophesy. And at Mizpah he receives the acclamation of the people who shout, *Long live the king!* (1 Samuel 10:24). Everything seems to be going fine, but after one year of reign he begins a downward spiral. It starts with impatience and presumption (1 Samuel 13:8–14) which leads to other disobedient acts and finally rejection by God (1 Samuel 15:11). He becomes a troubled man whose actions tend to be explosive and rash. His hatred explodes toward those that care for him the most. Jonathan, his son, and David, his servant, are the principal two who experience his rage and hostility (20:30–33). At the conclusion of his life, he is driven by jealousy and fear. This king who once prophesied in the name of the Lord now consults a witch for insight, and finally he commits suicide.

What a tragic end for such a promising beginning. Think about the people we know who come to the Lord and begin their lives in Christ with such promise. They are motivated and get involved with ministry, but somewhere along the way they become distracted. Their lives become driven by self-indulgence and a compromise of righteous standards. Soon, by choice, they isolate themselves from the people of God and begin to rationalize and justify their disobedient lives.

Others like Saul live under the illusion that because the power of God seems to be present and wonderful things happen because of them that they can live anyway they please. The day of reckoning comes and when they want a place in Christ's kingdom on the basis of their deeds, Jesus will say, *I never knew you* (Matthew 7:21–23).

Beginning well is good. Finishing well is better. Unlike Saul let us yearn for these words from the Savior, *Well done, good and faithful servant* (Matthew 25:21, 23).

Learning to Live Like a True King

One of the most beloved personalities of the Bible is David. The shepherd, psalmist, warrior, king was someone to admire. The uniqueness of David's life can be summed up in these words—he was a man after the Lord's own heart. No matter what would befall David he kept his heart tender toward God.

It all began with the visit of Samuel. The man of God had been commanded by the Lord to go to Bethlehem and anoint a new king. Saul was rejected as king and the prophet/judge goes to the house of Jesse as he was directed. It is this event that teaches us a very important lesson about God.

When the first of the sons of Jesse stands before Samuel, the prophet is rightly impressed. As he starts to anoint Eliab he is stopped by God and told not to anoint him. The lesson is that *man looks at the outward appearance, but the LORD looks on the heart* (1 Samuel 16:7).

David is called in from the field where he had been tending his father's flock of sheep. God makes it clear he is the one and after the oil is poured on his head, the Bible records that *the Spirit of the LORD came upon David from that day forward* (1 Samuel 16:13).

In the rest of the book of 1 Samuel David's life is intertwined with that of Saul, the disturbed and troubled king. The son of Jesse is called to serve Saul. His qualifications as reported in the Bible are these: *skillful in playing* (the harp), *a mighty man of valor, a man of war, prudent in speech, and a handsome person; and the LORD is with him* (1 Samuel 16:18).

The famous account of David's courage in facing the giant Goliath is one of the best known stories of Scripture (1 Samuel 17:1–58). This classic confrontation reveals the key to David's life. It is his confidence and trust in God. These two traits are seen clearly whether he is in battle, ruling the nation, or repenting of sin.

While the relationship with Saul deteriorates rapidly, one noble thing emerges. It is David's friendship with Jonathan, Saul's son. The bond between the two is an example of a deeply committed relationship that ultimately is expressed in Jonathan's acknowledging that one day David will be king instead of him, even though he is the king's heir. David in return promises to protect Jonathan's family forever.

Because of Saul's rage, David flees for his life and for a long period of years becomes a fugitive. Even though he is God's anointed king, he does not retaliate against Saul, God's rejected king.

It is during this "down" time of his life, living on the run, hiding in caves, and scavenging along the countryside, that David composes songs for the soul. Many have been collected and kept for us by the Holy Spirit in the book of the Psalms. Countless numbers of us have been comforted by this ancient poetry in times of our distress and confusion. They also reassure us of God's faithfulness and are a profound source of both the worship and praise of God our Savior.

During this time David has the occasion to put to the test what he values most. It is not the throne of Israel but the approval of God Almighty. And it is his trust in God and patience in His plan that makes David a great king. As a result God makes a covenant with him stating that a member of his family will be the eternal Anointed Redeemer, the Son of David, the Messiah, who will reign forever and ever (2 Samuel 7:8, 12, 16).

The book of 2 Samuel is the story of David's reign. For seven years he reigned in Hebron and for thirty-three years in Jerusalem after uniting the nation. His rule, however, was not without controversy.

His two most notable problems were his adultery with Bathsheba, including the murder of her husband Uriah, and the treason of his son Absalom. In both cases David faces his failure with contrition and humility. Psalm 51 is the record of his prayer of repentance over the Bathsheba episode. Nothing written about David is more important in helping us understand this great hero than his plea for forgiveness from and restoration with the Lord.

David demonstrates for us that it is not power or position that makes a regal person. His life illustrates that subjection to God in all things can make the most common of us a true king and servant of God.

And this royal reality is accomplished through

Christ, the Son of David, who loved us and washed us from our sins in His own blood, and made us kings and priests to His God and Father (Revelation 1:5b, 6a).

Learning Who Reigns

1 and 2 Samuel end with an insightful account of David facing another failure. His sin has an impact on the whole nation. In order to remove the plague of judgment, he is told by the prophet Gad to erect an altar to the Lord on the threshing floor of Araunah. Araunah offers to give David the site as well as the animals to sacrifice. King David replies that he will not offer to the Lord that which costs him nothing (2 Samuel 24:24). This action reveals that David the king has learned valuable life lessons through crushing experiences.

It is at this altar site that a worship act of allegiance to the King of Kings is performed. In so doing he acknowledges that no matter what our station in life we are still subservient to God as Regent. This act has prophetic implications too. For it is here a few years later that David's son Solomon will build the temple and it will be filled with the glory and presence of God (2 Chronicles 7:1).

A threshing floor seems to be an odd place for a sincere offering of sacrifice. The place is very symbolic, however, because as wheat is ground to offer its nutrients so life can grind us. And when the veneer of our flesh is removed we can offer our lives as living sacrifices which is our reasonable act of worship to King Jesus, Son of David, Savior of all.

Learning the lessons of these events recorded in

1 and 2 Samuel and **applying** them will give us the fortitude to overcome life's challenges. They will also enable us to navigate now in such a way that we may abide in God's forever kingdom.

I beseech you therefore, brethren,
by the mercies of God,
that you present your bodies
a living sacrifice, holy, acceptable
to God, which is your reasonable service
(Romans 12:1).

Using and Growing with the
BIBLE BOOK-A-MONTH STUDIES

The formulation of the ***Bible Book-A-Month*** concept was born in the heart of Dr. Jack Hayford to help people achieve three things: *systematic*, *substantial*, and *thorough* coverage of the Bible.

The Triangular Approach

There are many worthwhile approaches to a study of the Holy Bible—for example, "synthetic" study—which draws together highlights to provide a quick grasp of a book; "critical" study—which assesses the ancient textual resources that authenticate the trustworthiness of the book as a document; or "verse-by-verse" study—which seeks to exhaust every book of the totality of its content.

Distinct from any of these, the ***Bible Book-A-Month*** study seeks to achieve the maximum possible grasp of a book's truth, while keeping a pace forward which sustains the average Bible student's interest. It is <u>demanding</u> enough in its *academics* to seriously engage those interested in intelligent, thought-provoking study. Yet it is <u>dynamic</u> enough in its *movement* to avoid losing passion and to keep each student at a point of continuous anticipation.

This is done through use of a **"triangular**

approach" to each book—which focuses the three primary things to be found in every book of the Bible.

1. Each Bible book contains an *essential message*: the core concepts which distinguish that book and provide its place in God's Word.
2. Each Bible book presents *problems* and evokes *questions*. Good Bible study helps questioners find *satisfactory answers* to reasoned inquiry, even as it demonstrates the *relevancy* of God's Word and discovers the power of the Holy Spirit revealed in each book.
3. Each Bible book provides *practical wisdom* and *personal guidance*. In each book, *insights for faithful, fruitful pathways* will show how to adopt, adapt, and apply the Bible to your life, as Jesus' disciple.

Triple Tools—Support Resources
1. Each study is accented by a *pocket-sized book* as the one you have in hand.
2. Pastor Hayford is in the process of reading the whole Bible in the New King James Version on audio cassette. These can be ordered in conjunction with the *Bible Book-A-Month* program.
3. Overview teachings of each book are available on audio cassette as recorded live at The Church On The Way.

Additional resources, noted in each volume, can be ordered by calling Living Way Ministries at 818-779-8480 or 800-776-8180.

BIBLE BOOK-A-MONTH STUDY RESOURCES

STUDY PAK

The <u>Study Pak</u> on 1 and 2 Samuel includes this book and two tapes by Pastor Hayford. One tape is an overview of this study, and the second tape features Pastor Jack reading excerpts from the books of 1 and 2 Samuel.

SPSAM $12

STUDY ALBUM

The <u>Study Album</u> includes this 72-page printed overview of 1 and 2 Samuel along with three audio teachings by Drs. Hayford, Bauer, and Hamilton with an additional BONUS tape. **BBAM10 $15**

Call 1-800-776-8180 for information on other Bible Book-A-Month studies!

ABIDING IN THE ANOINTING

In this series of teachings Pastor Hayford presents biblical principles and precepts that will help every believer understand the true source of our spiritual authority and find spiritual power for effective service. He also shares what the Bible says about anointing, visions, defending against spiritual attacks, and how to stay connected to the Savior.

Audio: (4 tapes) **SC480** **$19**
Video: (2 VHS) **AIAVS** **$30**

HOW NOT TO LIVE LIKE A KING

Pastor Hayford teaches on the personal weaknesses of four of the Old Testament kings who reigned in Israel and Judah, and explains how we can learn from their obedience, their disobedience, and their failings.

Audio: (4 tapes) **SC520** **$20**
Video: (2 VHS) **NLKVS** **$30**

HAYFORD'S BIBLE HANDBOOK

Hayford's Bible Handbook is an unparalleled resource that uniquely unveils the keys to Scripture, providing not only a wealth of information, but also a spiritual stimulus that will encourage your faith and service to Christ.

It unlocks Scripture with:

- Illuminating surveys of each book of the Bible.
- Helpful illustrations, time lines, maps, and charts; plus an up-to-date discussion of archaeological discoveries that illustrate and verify bible accounts.
- A complete Visual Survey of the Bible.
- An Encyclopedic Dictionary with over 1,300 entries that address subjects of particular interest to Spirit-filled believers.

reg. $26.99 **HBH $22.99**

This guide opens the riches of Scripture to deepen your life in Christ.

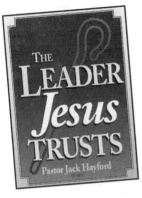